Taylor Swift

Country's S

An Unauthorized Biography by *Lexi Ryals*

PSS!
PRICE STERN SLOAN

PRICE STERN SLOAN
Published by the Penguin Group
Penguin Group (USA) Inc., 375 Hudson Street, New York, New York 10014, USA
Penguin Group (Canada), 90 Eglinton Avenue East, Suite 700,
Toronto, Ontario M4P 2Y3, Canada
(a division of Pearson Penguin Canada Inc.)
Penguin Books Ltd., 80 Strand, London WC2R 0RL, England
Penguin Group Ireland, 25 St. Stephen's Green, Dublin 2, Ireland
(a division of Penguin Books Ltd.)
Penguin Group (Australia), 250 Camberwell Road, Camberwell, Victoria 3124, Australia
(a division of Pearson Australia Group Pty. Ltd.)
Penguin Books India Pvt. Ltd., 11 Community Centre,
Panchsheel Park, New Delhi—110 017, India
Penguin Group (NZ), 67 Apollo Drive, Rosedale, North Shore 0632, New Zealand
(a division of Pearson New Zealand Ltd.)
Penguin Books (South Africa) (Pty.) Ltd., 24 Sturdee Avenue,
Rosebank, Johannesburg 2196, South Africa

Penguin Books Ltd., Registered Offices:
80 Strand, London WC2R 0RL, England

Photo credits: Cover: courtesy of Mark Humphrey/AP Photo; Insert photos:
first page courtesy of Jeff Adkins/AP Images; second page courtesy of Frank Mullen/
WireImage.com, WireImage.com; third page courtesy of Chris Gordon/WireImage.com,
Tammie Arroyo/AP Images; fourth page courtesy of Chris Pizzelo/AP Images.

Library of Congress Cataloging-in-Publication Data is available.

ISBN 978-0-8431-3347-9   10 9 8 7 6 5 4 3 2

❧ Table of Contents

Introduction

Seventeen-year-old Taylor Swift had butterflies in her stomach as she waited to take the stage at the 2007 Academy of Country Music Awards on the night of May 15, 2007. The room was packed with country music's elite, including George Strait, Kenny Chesney, LeAnn Rimes, Faith Hill, and Tim McGraw. Taylor had already watched some of her favorite singers accept their prestigious awards and was feeling a little starstruck to be a part of the country music world. She'd been working toward that night since she was eleven years old, and it almost didn't seem real now that she was finally there.

Wearing a white dress with feathers along the bottom and brown cowboy boots, Taylor walked onstage and slung her acoustic guitar over her shoulder. She listened nervously as presenter and actress Emma Roberts announced that Taylor Swift was dedicating her performance that night to Tim McGraw. Then the spotlight went up on Taylor and she began to play. She sang her heart out as she performed "Tim McGraw" off of her debut album, *Taylor Swift*. Taylor's single had been out for almost a year, but she had yet to meet the country star whose music had inspired it. That night Tim McGraw and his country-singer wife, Faith Hill, were both sitting front and center in the audience.

As Taylor let the last note of her song die away, she walked forward to Tim's seat and bent down to shake his hand. "Hi. I'm Taylor," she said, before giving him a huge hug. Tim was smiling ear to ear and so was Faith Hill, who also hugged Taylor. They both loved the song and Tim was honored that his music had inspired the newest generation of country singers. He had been looking forward to meeting Taylor, the precocious singer/songwriter who loved his music enough to make his name her song title, and there was no better place for such a meeting than at the Academy of Country Music Awards.

Taylor didn't win any awards that night, but that didn't matter to her. She had gotten to meet one of her favorite country stars, and she had blown the crowd away with her performance. It had been a whirlwind of a year for Taylor, who had gone from being an ambitious, talented schoolgirl living in Hendersonville, Tennessee, to a bona fide country music star. She had released her first single, which had made it to number 6 on the Billboard Hot Country chart, and her debut album had already been certified gold, selling over half a million copies. She was one of the most requested stars on country radio and was right in the middle of a six-month-long promotional radio tour. Life was good for country's newest golden girl, and although she didn't know it then, things were only going to get better.

Chapter 1
Country Girl

Long before she took the stage at the ACM Awards, Taylor was just a regular girl growing up in Pennsylvania.

When Scott and Andrea Swift got married, they moved to a small Christmas tree farm in Wyomissing, Pennsylvania, just outside of Reading. The newlyweds were ambitious and practical. Scott was a financial advisor for Merrill Lynch. "Business-wise, he's brilliant," Taylor proudly told the *Ottawa Citizen* about her father. In addition to being a supportive wife, Andrea was also a no-nonsense career woman focused on climbing the corporate ladder. "Before she [my mom] had me, she was this really big business executive that worked for an ad agency. I really look up to that. I respect that she had a career on her own and lived alone. She had me when she was 30. She had a complete career of her own and was supporting herself," Taylor told GACtv.com. Together, the two were very happy, but they wanted to start a family. So they were overjoyed when Andrea discovered she was pregnant with their first child in early 1989.

On December 13, 1989, the proud new parents welcomed a baby girl into the world. Andrea was ecstatic about the arrival of her daughter, and she had a very strong opinion about what her new baby's name should be. "She named me Taylor so that if anybody saw on a business card the name, Taylor, they wouldn't know if it was a girl or a guy if they were thinking of hiring me," Taylor explained to the *Toronto Star*. Andrea wanted to make sure that her daughter had every advantage should she decide to take on the business world; she just never thought it would be the music business that Taylor would conquer.

After Taylor was born, Andrea became a full-time mom—well, for most of the year anyway. Every December, Andrea would spearhead the Swift family's side business—selling Christmas trees from their farm. But she always saved the best tree for her own home! Taylor has always been glad that her mother was home when she was little. "My mom decided to stay home to raise me. She totally raised me to be logical and practical. I was brought up with such a strong woman in my life and I think that had a lot to do with me not wanting to do anything half-way," Taylor told the *Ottawa Citizen*. Andrea lavished her daughter with encouragement, making sure that baby Taylor flourished.

And flourish she did! "I was raised on a little farm and for me when I was little, it was the biggest place in the world. And it was the most magical, wonderful place in the world," Taylor explained to the *Ottawa Citizen*. Even from an early age, Taylor was determined. She was quick to decide what she wanted and go after it. All of the holiday visitors who came to buy trees were completely charmed by Taylor. And Taylor was fascinated by the visitors, too. Her mother told GACtv.com, "From day one, Taylor was always trying to figure out how other people thought and what they were doing and why they were doing it. That was probably an early telltale sign that she had the makings of a songwriter."

When Taylor was two, her mother announced that she was expecting again—Taylor was going to be a big sister! Taylor was probably pretty excited when her brother Austin was born. As the two siblings grew, they bonded quickly and loved playing games, watching cartoons, and goofing off together.

The Swifts loved life on the farm, but some of their favorite times as a family were their vacations to the beach in Stone Harbor, New Jersey. As Taylor explained to Searay.com, "At the age of four, I lived in a lifejacket. We've always been able to establish and maintain a family atmosphere even when we're far from home, and I think all those years going to the shore helped that."

Taylor and Austin soon grew into tall, energetic kids. They went to the Wyncroft School in Pottstown, Pennsylvania, for elementary school. Taylor excelled at

English and creative writing. She even won a national poetry contest when she was in fourth grade. Austin was a natural athlete, but despite a height advantage, Taylor was not. "Everybody thought I'd be good at basketball, but then I tried out and it was, like 'Oh.' I was awful at anything that's sports," Taylor explained to the *Ottawa Citizen.*

Luckily, Taylor was a natural at something else—performing. From a very early age, she loved to ham it up. By the time Taylor was two, she was already entertaining her family, their friends, and even strangers by singing. Her favorite songs to perform were tunes from Disney movies, as she told the *Philadelphia Inquirer.* "There are videos of me walking up to strangers and singing songs from *The Lion King* when I was a baby." Andrea and Scott probably weren't too surprised that they had a little songbird on their hands. Andrea's mother was a professional opera singer and Taylor seemed to have inherited her grandmother's gift for performing.

"My grandparents lived all over the world. In Puerto Rico, my grandmother was the hostess of the top-rated TV variety show called *The Pan-American Show*. Nanny's Spanish was so bad that the Puerto Ricans thought she was hysterically funny! She went on to become the 'madrina' [symbolic grandmother figure] of their Air Force; they really loved her. She starred in a lot of operas and was a member of the Houston Grand Opera. I think that's where I got most of my musical ability," Taylor told *Wood & Steel*. Taylor and her grandmother were very close and she was one of Taylor's biggest musical mentors.

Taylor's nanny wasn't the only musical influence in her life. When she was six, Taylor received her first LeAnn Rimes album, *Blue,* and discovered country music. She listened to that album nonstop and soon she could perform all of LeAnn's songs. LeAnn was one of the biggest teen country stars of all time, releasing her first album when she was only thirteen years old and making it into the record books as the first country artist ever to receive the Best New Artist Grammy Award. So it's no surprise that little Taylor wanted to follow in her footsteps. "I knew every song she ever sang. After that, I kind of went back and learned the history. I listened to legends like Dolly and Patsy Cline— women who were the essence of country music," Taylor told GACtv.com. Taylor was hooked on country music. "I was influenced early on by all of the great female country artists of the '90s and all of the cool music they were putting out. Like Shania, Faith, the Dixie Chicks. It was such great music, and it completely drew me in to country music," Taylor explained to CMT.com.

Taylor couldn't stop singing along to the country albums, so her mom encouraged her to try out for the community children's theater when she was nine. Taylor took to the stage immediately. She had a blast acting, but she loved performing in musicals the best. It was onstage at the theater that Taylor finally realized that being a country music singer was what she wanted to do for the rest of her life. "I was playing the role of Sandy in *Grease* and it just came out sounding country. It was all I had listened to so I guess it was just kind of natural. I decided country music was what I needed to be doing," Taylor told GACtv.com. Taylor wasn't the only one who noticed a decidedly country twang to her performance. As Andrea explained to Searay.com, everyone else realized it, too. When Taylor took the stage to belt out her big solo, "Hopelessly Devoted To You," another parent leaned in to Andrea and Scott and whispered, "You have a great little country singer there."

Once Taylor had performed in front of an audience, there was no going back. She loved being onstage under the bright lights, the rounds of applause, and, most of all, expressing herself through music. Taylor had always loved singing, but when she performed in front of a live audience she felt complete. She knew then that she wanted to be a professional singer. And not just any professional singer. Taylor wanted to be the next big country music star.

Chapter 2
Chasing The Dream

Once Taylor made up her mind to become the next country star, she got right to work chasing her big dream. Taylor already knew all of the words to her favorite country songs, so she started with karaoke performances. There were a few bars and restaurants in the area that hosted karaoke nights, and Taylor made sure she performed in every one of them she could. She really had to beg her parents to take her when the karaoke nights were in bars, which weren't necessarily the most appropriate places for a ten-year-old girl to be hanging out. "They [my mom and dad] were kind of embarrassed by it, I guess. This little girl singing in this smoky bar. But they knew how much it meant to me so they went along with it," Taylor explained to GACtv.com.

Eventually Scott and Andrea were won over by their daughter's enthusiasm and dedication and began helping her line up gigs, even in bars. "I think people should never ever put an age limit on what someone can accomplish. My parents, ever since the day I was born, have empowered me. There are really two ways to look at it when you are raising kids. You can either say 'You can be whatever you want to be' and then there is actually believing it. My parents actually believed it," Taylor told GACtv.com about her parents.

One of Taylor's favorite karaoke spots was the Pat Garrett Roadhouse. Pat Garrett is a country singer who had a few hits in the early 1980s and then settled down in Pennsylvania. In addition to his Roadhouse, Pat also owns and runs the Pat Garrett Amphitheater, where tons of country acts come to perform. Pat would sponsor karaoke nights a few times a week and would offer the winner a chance to open for whichever country act was performing at his amphitheater. "I started out singing karaoke in his [Pat Garrett's] roadhouse—his little bar—when I was 10 years old. He'll vouch that I was there every single week saying,

'I'm just going to come back if you don't let me win one.' I was kind of like an annoying fly around that place. I just would not leave them alone. What they would do is have these karaoke contests. And if you won, you got to open for, like, Charlie Daniels or George Jones. I would go until I would win," Taylor explained to CMT.com.

As a result of her determination and talent, Taylor got the chance to open for Charlie Daniels and several other country acts. She was nervous at first, especially since she was usually the only child performing! "I started singing in front of crowds when I was 10, and it was a little scary at first. Anything you've just started doing is going to be scary. Once, somebody told me to picture the audience in their underpants. Do *not* picture the audience in their underpants. That does not work. At all," Taylor told CMT.com. It turned out that her love of performing was all Taylor really needed to get over her nervousness.

Taylor's standout karaoke act quickly earned her a

reputation in the area, and she was soon performing at fairs and festivals throughout the state. Taylor jumped at every opportunity and impressed fair promoters and organizers with her professionalism and drive. "Every single weekend, I would go to festivals and fairs and karaoke contests—any place I could get up on stage. The cool thing about this is that my parents have never pushed me. It's always been [my] desire and love to do this. That's what makes this so sweet. If I had been pushed, if I didn't love this, I would probably not have been able to get this far," Taylor told CMT.com. Andrea and Scott were happy as long as Taylor was happy, and nothing made Taylor happier than singing in front of a crowd. So, while all of the other girls her age were having sleepovers, playing in pools, and hanging at the mall, Taylor was singing her heart out every weekend.

In addition to fairs and festivals, Taylor also sang the national anthem at a number of sporting events. One of her highest-profile gigs was performing at the start of a Philadelphia 76ers game, when a musical heavyweight just happened to be in the audience. "When I was 11, I sang the national anthem at a 76ers game in Philly. Jay-Z was sitting courtside and gave me a high five after I sang. I bragged about that for like a year straight," Taylor reminisced to CMT.com. Taylor had a lot of respect for the rap and hip-hop mogul and it was a huge compliment to have him recognize her ability—even if it was just a high five. It was certainly a sign that Taylor was more talented than your average eleven-year-old!

Riding high on successes like these, Taylor had her mother help her record a demo CD. It contained several tracks of Taylor singing karaoke to classic country songs. Taylor knew that if she wanted a record deal she was going to have to get the attention of the bigwigs of country music in Nashville, Tennessee. Nashville has long been the center of the country music world, which is why it's known as Music City. It's the home of the famed Ryman Auditorium, the Grand

Ole Opry, and Tootsie's Orchid Lounge. All of Taylor's favorite country artists had gotten their big breaks on Nashville's Music Row, a well-known street where every music label's offices are located. Since Taylor had her heart set on following in the boot prints of Patsy Cline, Faith Hill, LeAnn Rimes, and the Dixie Chicks, she and her mother made copies of her demo CD and drove down to Nashville. Taylor went into every music label, handed her demo to the receptionist, and said, "Hi. I'm Taylor. I'm eleven and I want a record deal." It took a lot of courage to put herself out there like that, especially knowing that most people who want to be stars never make it. But Taylor didn't let the thought of failure stop her. She believed in herself so much that she thought she would come home with a record deal for sure. As Taylor explained to GACtv.com, "I was like, if I want to sing music, I'm going to need a record deal. So, I'm going to get a record deal. I thought it was that easy. I made a demo tape of me singing along to karaoke songs and my mom and I started walking up and down Music Row handing them out to receptionists at every label. I think I had one person call me back. And he was so sweet, just kind of telling me, 'You know, this is not how you do this.'"

Taylor didn't get a recording contract on that trip to Nashville, but she did learn some valuable lessons. She went home to Wyomissing more determined than ever to break into country music. She learned that she needed to find a way to make herself stand out from the hundreds of other wannabe stars. After all, Taylor was young, beautiful, and had amazing singing and performing skills, but that wasn't enough when everyone she was competing with could claim the same thing. She just had to find what made her unique and try again.

All in all, things were going well for Taylor. She was performing as often as possible, and even though her first trip to Nashville hadn't gone exactly as planned, she had a much better idea of what she needed to work on to eventually score a record deal. So Taylor was pretty happy with life when she started seventh grade at Wyomissing Junior High School. She must have been excited to move to a bigger school with more opportunities for her to study music and tons of new classmates to perform for!

Unfortunately, Taylor was very disappointed with her new school. It seemed that her dedication to her craft and her musical success had alienated her from her classmates, and she suddenly found that her friends from elementary school wanted nothing more to do with her. "It was a really lonely time in my life," Taylor explained to the *Philadelphia Inquirer*. "I was friends with a group of girls, and then I wasn't friends with them anymore, and I didn't know why." Taylor was very hurt by the rejection of her peers and she couldn't figure out what she needed to say or do to get back in with the other kids. "I was not included. I would go to school some days, a lot of days, and not know who I was going to talk to. And that's a really terrifying thing for somebody who's 12," Taylor confessed to the *Toronto Star*.

Despite her troubles at school, Taylor tried to keep her spirits up. She threw herself into her music. Then one day when she was twelve, her computer, which she used to burn CDs of her demo, started acting up. So she called a repairman who turned out to be much more than a computer geek. "I learned to play guitar when this guy came over to fix my computer. He saw that I had [an acoustic guitar] in the corner, and he goes, 'Do you know how to play that? You want me to teach you some chords?' I was like, 'Yeah, sure!' So he taught me three chords," Taylor told GACtv.com. Taylor played those chords over and over until she had the feel of them. When she strummed that guitar, it was as if everything clicked into place. After the computer repairman left, Taylor sat down with her guitar in hand and wrote her first song using only those three cords. It was called "Lucky You."

Songwriting came naturally to Taylor, and she soon found that writing was the perfect way to express herself. She could pour out her emotions, events of the day, and her dreams into the music and lyrics and feel better, no matter how badly she had been feeling before. Performing her own songs was a completely different experience for Taylor. She felt like she was connecting with her audience on a new level, and she soon realized that the fact that she wrote and performed her own music was what could set her apart from other artists.

Freshly motivated by her newfound talent, Taylor set to work practicing guitar every chance she could get. She would rush home from school every day, race through her homework, and then practice. "I would be playing four hours a day until my fingers were bleeding and my mom called me to dinner," Taylor says in her official biography. As her playing skills grew, so did her collection of songs. One of her first was inspired by seeing LeAnn Rimes in concert and is called "Kid in the Crowd." Another of her early compositions is called "The Outside," and was one of several songs she wrote about feeling alienated from her classmates at school. "I found myself watching their reactions and their emotions mostly to figure out what I was doing so wrong. But then I realized if I could watch these people and write it all down, it would make a good song," Taylor explained to GACtv.com. Eighth grade hadn't been any better socially for Taylor than seventh had been. She was still alone most of the time and very few of the girls at school were even friendly to her. A lot of kids would have turned to destructive habits like drugs or alcohol to deal with those feelings of rejection and loneliness, but that was never an option for Taylor, no matter how bad things got. As she explained to the *Toronto Star*, "The thing that I found to escape from any pain . . . was writing songs."

Taylor's parents worried about their suddenly introverted daughter, and hearing the pain in her lyrics nearly broke their hearts. "When she started writing music, some of the first things she wrote about

[were] being unhappy and left out. But it was an outlet, so I was thrilled that she found a way to express it and let it go," Andrea told GACtv.com. But Taylor wouldn't trade those two difficult years for anything in the world, because it was going through that rejection that helped her find her voice in songwriting. As she explained to CMT.com, "I found that I was alone a lot of the time, kind of on the outside looking into their discussions, and the things they were saying to each other. They really didn't talk to me . . . I started developing this really keen sense of observation—of how to watch people and see what they did. From that sense, I was able to write songs about relationships when I was 13 but not in relationships."

Taylor continued to perform at festivals and fairs, singing her own songs and accompanying herself on her acoustic guitar. But she still sometimes sang an old classic, the national anthem, and that's the song that gave her one of her biggest breaks. Taylor was honored to be asked to belt out America's official song at the U.S. Open tennis tournament when she was thirteen. She gave it all she had, as always, and the audience took notice. "While I was singing the National Anthem, the entertainment director for the U.S. Open started asking my dad about me. Afterward, my dad put together this typical 'dad video' type of thing—with the cat chewing the neck of my Taylor [guitar], and stuff like that—and sent it to her, not knowing that she was going to send it to Dan Dymtrow. Dan called and asked us to come down and play for him in his office, so I brought my first 12-string down and played some songs for them. Dan said, 'I want to work with you guys,' and it's been great ever since! I love Dan—he is an awesome manager," Taylor told *Wood & Steel*. Dan Dymtrow was the then manager of pop superstar Britney Spears.

Dan got right to work promoting Taylor, and one of his first acts as her manager was to get her featured in the popular clothing store Abercrombie & Fitch's rising star campaign. That was a very proud moment for Taylor, who was already a huge fan of Abercrombie's cute distressed jeans, button-downs, and T-shirts. The trendy clothes were a big hit with the girls at Wyomissing Junior High, and Taylor probably felt a certain satisfaction when the girls who had snubbed her so badly saw Taylor highlighted in Abercrombie's advertising.

The Abercrombie campaign was just the beginning of Dymtrow's plans for Taylor's career. She recorded a new demo album featuring the best of her original songs, and Dymtrow made sure that all of the country music heavy hitters heard it. He shopped the demo around, and as a professional, he was able to get much more attention than Taylor had on her own. The Nashville music labels were intrigued by the young singer and songwriter, and were interested to hear her live. When Taylor headed back down to Nashville, she was surrounded by plenty of buzz. This time, Music Row took notice. After several meetings with different labels, RCA, which stands for Radio

Corporation of America, offered thirteen-year-old Taylor a development deal. A development deal meant that RCA was willing to give Taylor money, resources, and studio time to record songs, with no guarantee that they would put out an album. It wasn't quite a record deal, but it was an amazing opportunity for Taylor. The only problem was that RCA was located in Nashville, and Taylor and her family lived in Wyomissing, Pennsylvania. Taylor and her mother took a few trips to Nashville to meet with RCA's songwriters and producers, but it became increasingly difficult to take advantage of RCA's resources from so far away. So, after some soul-searching, Taylor and her family decided to make the move to Nashville so that Taylor could really pursue her career. The Swifts were goin' country—for real!

Chapter 3
Music City Here She Comes

Taylor was thrilled about her family's big move. She was ready to leave the difficult years of junior high behind her and really get started pursuing her big dreams in the city where country was king—Nashville, Tennessee. She was sad to leave behind her childhood home and all of her fans from her regular appearances at festivals, fairs, and karaoke hot spots, but she knew it was worth it. Luckily, Taylor's family was supportive enough of her dreams to make the move for her. "Andrea and Taylor had been road-tripping to Nashville a lot for songwriting and recording sessions, and we realized it might make sense to move," Scott told Searay.com.

The Swifts wanted to wait until school let out for the summer to make the actual move, but Andrea began house hunting on their regular trips down to Nashville throughout the spring. Andrea knew she had found the perfect place when she toured an adorable house right on Old Hickory Lake in Hendersonville. Hendersonville is a suburb of Nashville. It's close to the big city, but still had the small-town charm the Swifts were looking for. The rest of the family fell in love with the lake—especially Scott, who told Searay.com, "When Andrea found a place on Old Hickory Lake, we stopped at the dock on the way up to check out the house. I looked down the cove toward the lake, imagined my Sea Ray tied up there and said, 'I'll take it.' She said, 'Don't you want to see the house first?'" The Swifts were in good company in their new home. Music legend Roy Orbison had a home on Old Hickory Lake for twenty years; country's "Man in Black" himself, Johnny Cash, and his wife, June Carter Cash, lived on the lake in an eighteen-room mansion until their deaths in 2003; and Richard Sterban of the Oak Ridge Boys lived nearby. Maybe there's something in that Old Hickory Lake water that helps produce hits!

Once they found their dream home, the Swifts packed up and moved over the summer. Both Taylor and Austin adjusted to life in Tennessee pretty quickly. When school started in the fall, Austin became involved in athletics, excelling at football, and found a great group of friends. Taylor was also finally having luck at school. Hendersonville High School was a fresh start for the one-time outsider. Despite her single-minded focus on music after school, during the school day, Taylor began to find her balance socially. In her freshman-year English class, Taylor clicked with a girl named Abigail Anderson and they became fast friends. "We became best friends right away . . . we went through just about everything together," Taylor told GACtv.com. The two girls often got in trouble for being silly in class, and they drove Taylor's parents nuts giggling at their inside jokes. "Me and [my] friend, Abigail, always talk with Minnesota accents and everyone thinks we're weird. When I was in ninth grade, (we) didn't talk in any other voice except *Napoleon Dynamite* the entire year," Taylor explained to the *St. Petersburg Times*. It was nice for Taylor to finally have a best friend, especially after all of those friendless years in junior high. Abigail had no musical aspirations of her own, but she was always super supportive and remains one of Taylor's biggest fans. Not all of Taylor's new classmates understood Taylor, as she explained to GACtv.com. "I sang country music. I played guitar. In class I would sit there writing down lyrics. And I don't think they got that, really." But they were all impressed by her musical abilities, which she showcased in music classes and school assemblies, and they all thought it was pretty cool to have a budding country star in their midst. "Music has always been my game," Taylor explained to Searay.com. "It's my after-school activity. Everyone at school knows it's what I do and they're all really supportive."

Some of Taylor's classmates were bigger fans than others, especially the boys at Hendersonville High!

Taylor had always felt out of place and awkward in Wyomissing, but she blossomed in Nashville and the local boys took notice. She had always been confident about her music, but changing schools and interacting with different kids had helped Taylor gain confidence in herself, including her looks. And, at 5'11" without shoes, Taylor literally stood out in a crowd. She began showing off her slender build and long legs more by wearing lots of dresses and skirts. She stopped trying to straighten her blond curls and, instead, grew them even longer, adopting the signature hairstyle that her fans have come to love. Taylor began talking and flirting with boys, and soon she was going on dates and getting boyfriends.

One of Taylor's boyfriends, Brandon Borello, inspired Taylor to write "Our Song." Taylor and Brandon, a senior, had been struggling to find a song that described their relationship perfectly—but nothing seemed to fit. When Taylor needed a new song to perform at the Hendersonville High talent show, she decided to write one for her and her boyfriend. Taylor's incredibly catchy love song was the hit of the talent show. As she explained to Music.aol.com, "I wrote this song in my freshman year of high school for my ninth grade talent show. I was sitting there thinking, 'I've gotta write an upbeat song that's gonna relate to everyone.' And at that time, I was dating a guy and we didn't have a song. So I wrote us one, and I played it at the show. Months later, people would come up to me and say, 'I loved that song that you played.' And then they'd start singing lines of it back to me. They'd only heard it once, so I thought, 'There must be something here!'"

Taylor may have been shining at Hendersonville High School, but things weren't going as well at RCA. Taylor had been working hard to impress the executives at RCA, but they were still hesitant to put their full weight behind the fourteen-year-old by producing a record for her. They weren't impressed with Taylor's songs, and wanted her to record other people's songs instead, which wasn't what Taylor wanted for herself. She wanted more attention and direction than the label was willing to give her. As she told *Entertainment Weekly,* "I did not want to be on a record label that wanted me to cut other people's stuff. That wasn't where I wanted to be . . . I didn't want to just be another girl singer. I wanted there to be something that set me apart. And I knew that had to be my writing. Also, it was a big, big record label with big superstars, and I felt like I needed my own direction and the kind of attention that a little label will give you. I just did not want it to happen with the method of 'Let's throw this up against the wall and see if it sticks, and if it doesn't, we'll just walk away.' I wanted a record label that needed me, that absolutely was counting on me to succeed." So, after a year of development, Taylor walked away from RCA and began shopping her demos around to the major labels again. She also parted ways with her manager Dan Dymtrow.

It was a challenging and frustrating time for Taylor—but she handled it with her usual combination of grace, strength, and persistence. "Being able to face the rejections of Nashville is nothing compared to facing the rejections at middle school," Taylor told the *Miami Herald*. Taylor had her work cut out for her, as she explained to *Entertainment Weekly*. "It's not a really popular thing to do in Nashville, to walk away from a major record deal. But that's what I did, because I wanted to find some place that would really put a lot of time and care into this." That only meant that Taylor had to work extra hard to convince Nashville's major labels to take a chance on her. She met with executive after executive, but they were all wary about making an album with a fourteen-year-old, no matter how talented. Other country stars had started very successful careers in their teens, such as LeAnn Rimes, Dolly Parton, and Tanya Tucker, but even more had failed. "I can understand," Taylor told CMT.com. "They were afraid to put out a 13-year-old. They were afraid to put out a 14-year-old. Then they were afraid to put out a 15-year-old. Then they were nervous about putting out a 16-year-old."

Luckily, Taylor didn't give up. She kept pushing for what she wanted, and she was talented enough to get it. Sony/ATV certainly took notice of the pretty fourteen-year-old and her original compositions. They didn't offer Taylor a record deal, but they did offer her a job. They signed Taylor on to a publishing deal as a house writer, the youngest house writer in their history. Taylor was thrilled to have someone recognize her for her songwriting talents and she couldn't wait to get to work.

Chapter 4
The Write Stuff

Taylor was thrilled to begin her after-school job, but she knew she was going to have to work harder than every other songwriter at Sony. Being a good fourteen-year-old writer wouldn't be enough—Taylor was determined to be one of the best songwriters of any age, but she was also determined to keep working toward getting her own record out. "I signed my publishing deal at age 14 with Sony/ATV," Taylor explained to songwriteruniverse.com. "I signed and worked with (exec) Arthur Buenahora, who was great. When I signed, I knew that I had to work just as hard as the veteran 45-year-old writers who were also signed there. I wrote a lot of songs, which were mainly for my own artist project, rather than writing songs for pitching to other artists." When Taylor finally got the chance to record her own album, she wanted to make sure she was ready—with enough single-worthy tunes to fill her debut ten times over! Of course, Taylor was allowed to keep any of the songs she wrote for herself, but if it was a song she knew she wouldn't record, other artists could consider it for their albums. With that kind of motivation, her bosses never had to push her. Taylor pushed herself harder than anyone else ever could have.

Taylor used her age and her experiences to her advantage when it came to her songwriting—she wrote what she was feeling as a young teenage girl, hoping that other teenage girls could relate. As she explained to the *Ontario Star*, "I think I've been inspired by things that have actually happened. I can't sit down and write about something I've never felt before. The songs I write in 15 minutes—because they're just so fast, they just come to me—are about things I've gone through." For Taylor, songwriting was better than going to therapy. "Whatever you're feeling that day, it comes out of you. It's kind of like photography—looking at a little picture album of where you are emotionally. I now consider myself a songwriter first and foremost, and I have never written anything I didn't mean," Taylor explained to GACtv.com. Of course, not every song she wrote was up to her incredibly high standards. She often spent days editing a song, only to put it away knowing she would never record it. Even if Taylor knew she wouldn't use a song, she still wanted to finish what she had started to the best of her ability.

Taylor's greatest source of inspiration was in her high school. She often wrote about her classmates, and she was never shy about including personal details. She likes calling people out in her music, especially when it comes to boys who break her heart. "When you go through a horrible breakup—from someone you should never have dated in the first place—it's a waste of effort. But if you write a song about the experience it's not a wasted experience, it helped the career," Taylor explained to the *Miami Herald*.

Taylor doesn't let any experience go to waste—she even writes songs about boys she didn't date, or wants to date, or boys who break her friends' hearts. "You listen to my [songs] and it sounds like I've had 500 boyfriends. But that's really not the case. I found that you don't have to date someone to write a song about them," Taylor explained to CMT.com.

Sometimes Taylor found that inspiration hit at the worst possible times—like in the middle of class. "Writing a song . . . you don't feel like you're really doing it. You feel like the song is coming to you, sometimes, and you can't really choose when that happens. I used to be at school and my teachers and classmates would all think I was weird because I would have to get up and go to the bathroom and record a melody into my phone so I could remember it," Taylor told the *St. Petersburg Times*. And boring classes were just more chances to polish her craft, as Taylor told GACtv.com. "If we had random notebook checks, my teachers might find biology notes . . . biology notes . . . then suddenly a bunch of lyrics." Luckily Taylor was such a good student that it didn't hurt her grades if she spent a little bit of time writing songs during class.

To help their newest employee perfect her songs and hone her songwriting skills, Sony paired Taylor up with one of their veteran songwriters, Liz Rose. In over twenty years in the business, Liz had never met anyone like Taylor. "She's probably the finest singer-songwriter I've ever worked with," Liz told the *Associated Press*. "She's a genius, coming in with ideas and a melody. She'd come in and write with this old lady, and I never second-guessed her. I respect her a lot." Liz and Taylor wrote together once a week, and Liz came to look forward to those writing sessions as her easiest of the week. "She always came in with an idea. Most of her songs are about something she has just gone through that day or that weekend. She is so fast and so good. But it's not that she's in a hurry. It's that she's got to get it *out*," Liz told GACtv.com.

Liz was apprehensive at first about working with such a young partner, but she was pleasantly surprised by Taylor's professional attitude. "We wrote every

Tuesday at four in the afternoon. She'd blow into the office and you'd hear about her day at school—this is what happened to some girl or some guy. She'd grab a handful of chocolate, walk into the writer's room, and shut the door. Until she got into that room, she was teenager. But once that door closed—she was a writer," Rose told GACtv.com. The two quickly developed a friendship, despite the difference in their ages. "I love writing with Liz," Taylor gushed to songwriteruniverse.com. "When we write, I usually come in with a melody and some lyric content, and then we'll work on creating the rest of the song. She's a really good song editor." Taylor claims she could never have written her hit songs without Liz, but Liz disagrees. "I laugh when people call me a cowriter. I just take dictation," Liz laughingly told GACtv.com.

One of the first songs Liz and Taylor worked on together was a bittersweet love song about Taylor's boyfriend Brandon Borello. Brandon was a senior and was getting ready to leave for college and Taylor knew their relationship was soon going to end. "I wrote [the song] in my freshman year of high school. I got the idea in math class. I was just sitting there, and I started humming this melody. I kind of related it to this situation I was in. I was dating a guy who was about to go off to college. I knew we were going to break up. So I started thinking about all the things that I knew would remind him of me. Surprisingly, the first thing that came to mind was that my favorite country artist is Tim McGraw," Taylor told CMT.com. "Tim McGraw" became the name of the tune and Taylor burst into her Tuesday meeting with Liz ready to get it on paper. As Liz told GACtv.com, "With 'Tim McGraw' she came in with the idea and melody. She knew exactly what she wanted." Writing about their impending split really helped ease the pain of saying good-bye for Taylor. Brandon was Taylor's first long-term boyfriend and they meant a lot to each other, but they knew it would be crazy to try to make a long-distance relationship work. "I dated him for about a year and we are still friends . . . He really thought it was cool that, [even though] we weren't going out anymore, I remembered our relationship nicely," Taylor told GACtv.com. That song, and that breakup, would turn out to be one of the best things to ever happen to Taylor. When Taylor did finally get a record deal, "Tim McGraw" would be her first single.

Taylor also wrote her second single, "Teardrops on My Guitar," with Liz's help. At the beginning of her sophomore year, Taylor had a huge crush on one of Hendersonville High's star wrestlers, Drew Hardwick. They were friends, but Drew had no idea how Taylor felt about him, as Taylor explained to *Country Standard Time*. "I used to have a huge crush on this guy, Drew, who would sit there every day talking to me about another girl: how beautiful she was, how nice and smart and perfect she was. I sat there and listened and said, 'Oh, I'm so happy for you.' I guess this is a good example of how I let my feelings out in songs and sometimes no other way. I love this song because of its honesty and vulnerability. To this day, Drew and his girlfriend are still together." Giving Drew advice on how to woo the girl of his dreams was agony for Taylor. She struggled with her crush for most of her sophomore year and was relieved to pour her feelings out into a song. With Liz's help, Taylor managed to capture exactly how she was feeling, and there are plenty of girls out there who could relate to that.

Taylor penned the angry country rock tune "Picture to Burn" about another guy who was never her boyfriend. "We almost dated. It really bothered me that he was so cocky and that's where that song came from. After school, I would write songs every single day, exactly what I felt. I found myself just sitting there with my guitar going, 'I hate his stupid truck that he doesn't let me drive. He's such a redneck! Oh my God!' That actually became the chorus to the song, so that's one of the most honest songs I've ever written," Taylor told GACtv.com. Taylor wrote one final breakup song a week before her final recording session when she found out that the boy she was dating, Sam, had cheated on her. Taylor isn't the type of girl to let something like that slide, so she immediately ended the relationship and put her anger into the song, "Should've Said No." "Basically, it's about a guy who cheated on me and shouldn't have because I write songs," she told CMT.com. Sam probably regrets cheating on Taylor now!

But not all of her songs are about romantic love. "There's one [song] on the album called 'Tied Together With a Smile' that I wrote about one of my friends, who is this beauty queen, pageant princess—a gorgeous, popular girl in high school. Every guy wanted to be with her, every girl wanted to be her. I wrote that song the day I found out she had an eating disorder," Taylor told *Entertainment Weekly*. Taylor was devastated that such a beautiful girl could have so little self-confidence. The girl has since gotten help and is doing much better, but Taylor hates that any girl could feel that way. If it was up to her, every girl would feel beautiful and special all of the time, and she hopes that her songs empower her fans.

While she was writing for Sony, Taylor was introduced to a demo producer named Nathan Chapman. Nathan and Taylor clicked immediately and the two worked closely together to create demos of the songs Taylor was writing. "I started off with this demo producer who worked in a little shed behind this publishing company I was at. His name was Nathan Chapman. I'd always go in there and play him some new songs, and the next week he would have this awesome track, on which he played every instrument, and it sounded like a record. We did this for a period of a year to two years before I got my record deal," Taylor told CMT.com.

Taylor developed a real rapport with Nathan and it showed in how well her demos came out. Those demos began to catch the attention of record executives on Music Row. Since Sony hadn't offered Taylor a record deal, she continued working for them as a songwriter, but kept taking her demos to different label executives. They were all watching Taylor, waiting to see how her skills would develop as she grew up. One executive in particular, Scott Borchetta, was especially interested in Taylor, but he was waiting for the right moment to make his move. Scott invited Taylor to his office at DreamWorks, where he was a Senior Vice President of Promotion and Artist Development. She played him a few of her songs live and he was very impressed with what he heard. "Still to this day, it never hit me that Taylor was a teenager. To me, she was a hit songwriter," Scott told CMT.com. Scott was gearing up to revolutionize the country music scene, and he had a feeling there was a perfect place for Taylor in his vision.

Chapter 5
A Little Bluebird Told Her . . .

Taylor spent the summer after her freshman year of high school gearing up for a very important songwriters showcase at Nashville's famous Bluebird Café. The Bluebird Café has a well-deserved reputation for launching country stars, like Garth Brooks. Everyone who's anyone in the Nashville music scene flocks to the Bluebird for the chance to see the first public performance of a future star or hit songwriter. As the youngest performer that night, Taylor stood out. "It was kind of an intimidating scene," Taylor told the *Denver Westword.* But Taylor was more than ready for that performance, and she proved to everyone in the room why she was there.

One audience member in particular was paying special attention to Taylor's performance. Scott Borchetta had met with Taylor several weeks before her showcase. He was already impressed with Taylor, but he was blown away by her stage presence and charisma at the Bluebird. "Out of all the people in the room, he was the only one who had his eyes closed and was totally into the music," Taylor told GACtv. com. Taylor never could have guessed the real reason he was there.

Scott wasn't looking to sign Taylor to DreamWorks. He wanted to sign Taylor to a new label, one he was about to create. Scott certainly had the experience to run his own label, having guided the careers of some of Music City's biggest stars including Toby Keith, George Strait, Reba McEntire, Trisha Yearwood, Shania Twain, Sugarland, and Lee Ann Womack. Still, Scott's plan was a huge risk for everyone involved.

A few weeks later, Taylor received a very mysterious phone call from Scott. "He was like, 'I'm going to be doing something and I need to talk to you in person because I don't trust the phone. And I was like, 'If you don't trust the phone there has got to be something going on that I want to know about.' And when I heard what he wanted to do, it absolutely blew my mind," Taylor told GACtv.com. Scott officially offered Taylor the first contract with his new independent label, Big Machine Records. Taylor was ecstatic to finally have a recording contract, and she was especially excited that it was with a new label, as she explained to GACtv.com. "That's always been my kind of thing. I've wanted to stir it up. I've always wanted people to say, 'Okay, she's doing things a little differently.'" Scott and Taylor were a perfect match and they didn't waste any time getting started.

Big Machine Records was up and running within a couple of months, and that fall Taylor signed her recording contract in a special ceremony at the Country Music Hall of Fame in downtown Nashville. Signing that contract was a big moment for Taylor. "It's kind of like a wedding contract," Taylor joked. But Scott wasn't joking when he answered, "No, it's more binding." After the signing, Scott took Taylor and her family out for a celebratory dinner at The Palm restaurant. Taylor had just signed up for the ride of a lifetime and she was ready to enjoy it.

Once the celebration was over, Taylor and Scott got down to business in the recording studio. Taylor had kept plenty of the songs she'd written at Sony for herself, so she had lots of material to work with. Taylor presented all of them to her new label president, and Scott was absolutely in awe of her talent. "I've never seen anything like it, to be honest with you. There's something about her songwriting that's just extraordinary. She has this amazing filter. Everyday life comes in and it comes out Taylor Swift music. I've had the good fortune to be working with a lot of great songwriters. And I'll put her in the room with anybody," he told GACtv.com.

In the end, Taylor and Scott chose three songs that Taylor had written on her own and eight that she had cowritten, including "Tim McGraw." "We played it for Scott, the president of my label, on a fluke—'Hey!

Listen to this song I wrote called 'Tim McGraw.' He looked at me and said, 'That's your first single.' I'm like, 'Well. *That's* how that works, then.' It never really occurred to me that the song would be so relatable," Taylor told GACtv.com. It was very important to her that her albums contained only music she had written and Scott agreed completely. Once the songs were chosen, it was time to record. It took four months to finish the album, and the process wasn't without its ups and downs. Taylor liked the producers and writers she had been working with at Sony, especially her demo producer Nathan Chapman, and was a little thrown off by working with new people who didn't know and understand her, no matter how talented they were. "We switched [album] producers a bunch of times," Taylor explained to CMT.com. "Then, all of a sudden, it was, 'Okay, we're going to use this producer,' or, 'We're going to use that producer.' So I got to record with a bunch of really awesome producers in Nashville. But it didn't sound the way that it did with Nathan. He had never made an album before. He had just recorded demos. But the right chemistry hit. Finally my record label president said, 'OK, try some sides with Nathan.'" In the end, Nathan produced all but one of the tracks on Taylor's debut and she couldn't have been happier with the final result.

Once the tracks were all recorded, the album still had to be mixed and the finishing touches, like the album cover and promotional materials, had to be added. Taylor tried to be patient, but she was anxious to present her masterpiece to the world. Scott began building the buzz about Taylor's debut all over town, and by June he felt the time was finally right to release her first single, "Tim McGraw." Taylor's life would never be the same.

Chapter 6
MySpace Princess

After all of her hard work in the studio, Taylor wanted the world to hear her album, but she had a long wait before the release date. Taylor has never been one to take it easy and she felt like she needed to do something productive while she was waiting. All of her friends at school were hooked on the online social networking site MySpace and Taylor thought it might be a good idea to create a profile for herself as a country music artist. Lots of musicians, bands, and singers create profiles on the site where fans can sample their music and check in for concert dates and news. Fans can then request to be added as friends of the artist and leave comments and feedback. Taylor knew she and her friends liked to spend hours online checking out new music, so she thought MySpace was a great way to get in touch with potential fans. The only problem was that there just weren't very many country artists online and Taylor wasn't sure if anyone would even find her profile. Still, she was determined to at least try.

Knowing the types of things that she and her friends checked out and responded to on MySpace, Taylor designed her profile. She wrote her biography in the first person, added all of the tracks from her album, pictures and video clips, a schedule of promotional events, and links to her official websites. She even added a girly pink floral background as the finishing touch. "I wrote it about who I am as a person. I have never been afraid to let people in to see that part of me, that I actually am a human being," Taylor explained to the *Tennessean*. After building her profile, Taylor began to watch it fanatically. She added all of her friends and classmates as MySpace friends and waited. Soon friends of friends began requesting to be her friend because they had clicked on her page and enjoyed her music. Taylor couldn't believe it.

Every time she checked her page there were more and more friend requests waiting for her and more and more people had listened to her songs. "I'm a MySpace freak," Taylor admitted to GACtv.com. "I'm absolutely obsessed with it." Taylor was thrilled that people were responding so favorably to her music, especially people her own age. As she explained to the *Tennessean*, "It's cool because my fans are all ages. Of course, there are a lot of them that are my age. That is so flattering to me because I know how picky I am about music and how picky my friends are about music. They are ruthless. But if they like something, they are so passionate and loyal. That is why I am so happy to have fans that are my age."

As her list of MySpace fans grew, they began clamoring for their own copies of her catchy songs. Taylor had over 2 million hits on her profile before her debut album was even released. In June, when "Tim McGraw" hit the airways, it was downloaded over 500,000 times in under five months. Taylor chalks it all up to her MySpace fan base, since it took a while for her single to break into country radio playlists. "I think MySpace has worked so well because I didn't want to make (my page) like every other artist's page, with a third-person bio that was completely not personal. Instead of doing that, I wrote a first-person bio about what I like and dislike. It is about what I am as a person, not my accomplishments. It lets them in and lets them know it's me running it, not a company. I love the fact that people my age are paying attention to my music. I know how my friends and I look at music and address music, either they love something or don't like it at all," she explained to the *Pantagraph*. Once *Taylor Swift* hit store shelves, the number of Taylor's MySpace friends shot through the roof as fans searched the Internet for more information on their favorite new singer.

Taylor's openness and personal approach on her profile helps fans feel like they really know her and are important to her—and they are. Taylor checks her page daily and tries to answer as many fan e-mails as possible. Before her album was released and her life became a whirlwind, Taylor would respond to about one hundred e-mails and postings a day. Andrea and Scott Swift would often have to force Taylor to turn off her computer and go to bed at night, and Taylor still felt she wasn't doing enough to respond to her fans. As she explained to GACtv.com, "My fans have done so much for me and have been pulling for me from the very beginning. It kills me that I can't go out to every single person in some way and say thank you so much and shake their hand." Her fans really relate to Taylor's songs and want to share with her how much her music had touched them. "They come on [MySpace] and tell their life story or why this song has meant so much to them. They're sharing their lives with Taylor," Andrea told GACtv.com.

The country music industry certainly took notice when teenage Taylor burst onto the scene with a ready-made fan base that already knew all of the words to her songs. The studios were blown away by the number of people Taylor had connected with using only her home computer. Lots of older music executives were especially puzzled, but Taylor knew exactly why MySpace had worked so well for her. As she explained to the *Tennessean*, "I nurtured it and really paid attention to it, like it was something important and not just a marketing tool." And Taylor wasn't just appealing to the traditional country fans—she was bringing a whole new generation into the fold, something country's bigwigs had been struggling to do for quite a while. "I think one of the cool things about this is that MySpace is one of the main reasons I'm here, along with radio and word of mouth. And MySpace is pretty much a younger thing, at the moment . . . So yeah, definitely, it's bringing a completely different audience to country music. And I am so grateful for that. I don't know what I did to make that happen, because everybody was talking about it. I would go to CRS [Country Radio Seminar] before I was ever signed to a record deal, and I would listen to people say, 'Someone needs to bring in that younger demographic.' And what I'm hearing is that we've done that, and we kind of stumbled upon it. I wasn't trying to be exclusive as to who would like it," Taylor told *Entertainment Weekly*.

For Taylor, who had grown up with computers and the Internet, using her computer to access music is second-nature, and she feels that kids her age are more open-minded about trying out new and different types of music since they can download just about any song out there for under a dollar. "In this day of iPods and digital and Internet and the fact people can go get any music they want with the click of a button, I really think there are less boundaries and the lines are more blurred between genres. And I think that's a beautiful thing," Taylor told the *Ontario Star*.

It's been well over two years since Taylor's MySpace profile went up and she is still dominating the site. She is ranked number 15 for the most

MySpace visits in all genres of music and is number one for the number of visits for a country artist, outdistancing other country artists by millions of hits. Fans have streamed songs off of her profile more than 35 million times. Radio airplay is great, but with Taylor's fans coming directly to her MySpace for music, it isn't as necessary as it once was. The Internet has completely revolutionized the music business for most genres of music—country is just one of the last genres to realize it. "People haven't fallen out of love with music. They've fallen in love with new ways to use it," Scott Borchetta said to the *Philadelphia Inquirer*. And that's just fine with Taylor. She loves being so accessible to her fans, and can't wait for MySpace to develop new ways for her and other musicians to get their music out there.

Chapter 7
Taylor Takes Off

It took Taylor forever to fall asleep on the night of June 5, 2006. The next day, June 6, her debut single "Tim McGraw" was going to be officially released. It had been up on her MySpace page for months and fans loved it, but Taylor was still nervous. She was also excited to hear herself on the radio, and hoped that Nashville's radio stations wouldn't bash all of her hard work on air. She had nothing to worry about.

"Tim McGraw" hit the airwaves the next day and immediately began racing up the Billboard Hot Digital Songs chart, which includes music from all genres. It would eventually peak at number 33 on that chart— which is pretty high for a country single. It took a little longer for "Tim McGraw" to really break into the notoriously tight country radio rotations. Country fans are known for being a little resistant to accepting new artists, but once they do, an artist is usually in for life. Scott warned Taylor it might take some time, so she tried to be patient. The first time Taylor heard her song on the radio, she was in her car with friends and family. A Nashville radio station played two new singles and then asked listeners to vote for their favorites. One was "Tim McGraw" and the other was a new song by Tim's wife, Faith Hill. Faith is a well-established country superstar and Taylor just knew she would lose, but, to her surprise, fans liked her song best! Faith probably didn't mind losing to a song with her husband's name in the title.

Luckily, Taylor was much too busy to worry about her chart standings. As soon as school let out, she set out on a six-month-long radio tour to promote "Tim McGraw" and her debut album, *Taylor Swift*. "Radio tours for most artists last six weeks. Mine lasted six months. That's because I wanted it to. I wanted to meet every single one of the people that was helping me out," she explained to CMT.com. Taylor wasn't at all shy about getting into every single radio station and convincing DJs that her music was worth playing. For the most part, the DJs were charmed by Taylor and her genuine enthusiasm, and she made friends at every station she stopped into. Being on the road was grueling, but Taylor cherished every minute of it—after all, she'd been working toward having an album to promote since she was ten years old—and she wasn't about to complain.

Taylor did take a break from the tour in October when Big Machine Records finally released *Taylor Swift*. It was a very big and emotional moment for Taylor, and it was definitely the highlight of her year. She was in New York City for the big day and was so excited that she went out and bought a copy of her own album that afternoon. Then she went home to Nashville for a few days to celebrate with her family and visit her friends. Taylor had decided to begin homeschooling so she could throw herself into her music career, but she missed seeing her friends every day, especially her best friend Abigail. But they were all so happy for her that they almost didn't mind her being gone so much—and they were some of the first people to run out and buy *Taylor Swift*.

Thanks to the momentum Taylor had built up promoting "Tim McGraw," her album sold steadily and began climbing the Billboard charts. It went gold by February 2007, only four short months after its release. Sony BMI threw their favorite songwriter a party so that Taylor could accept her gold album plaque in style. Taylor wore a sparkling gold dress in honor of the occasion and celebrated with a mix of Nashville music industry insiders, Hendersonville High School students and teachers, and family and close friends. It wasn't just the first gold album for Taylor—it was also the first gold album for Big Machine Records and Nathan Chapman, Taylor's producer. Scott Borchetta, Big Machine's president, was elated by the achievement, but he was also keeping his fingers crossed for more. He wore a platinum tie to the event to symbolize the next milestone he was hoping Taylor would achieve.

With her album doing well, "Tim McGraw" began to get a lot more airplay and started creeping up the charts itself. It eventually reached number 6 on Billboard's Hot Country Songs, number 43 on Billboard's Pop 100 chart, and number 40 on the Billboard Hot 100 chart. Taylor's songs were achieving something that few country songs ever do; it was being embraced by the music world outside of the country scene. "I think the reason why 'Tim McGraw' worked out was it was reminiscent, and it was thinking about a relationship that you had and then lost. I think one of the most powerful human emotions is what should have been and wasn't. I think everyone can relate to that. That was a really good first song to start out on, just because a lot of people can relate to wanting what you can't have," Taylor told *Entertainment Weekly*.

It seemed like the time was right to spin another single off of the album, and Scott Borchetta thought

"Teardrops on My Guitar" was the perfect choice. As soon as it was released, "Teardrops" shot up the charts, eventually hitting number 2 on the Billboard Hot Country Songs chart in August, number 11 on the Billboard Hot Digital Songs chart and the Pop 100 charts, number 14 on the Billboard Hot 100 chart, and number 17 on the Billboard Hot Adult Contemporary chart. In January 2008, "Teardrops on My Guitar" became the fourth digital platinum single in country music history, meaning that over 1 million people had downloaded the single. Carrie Underwood, Rascal Flatts, and the Dixie Chicks are the only other artists to ever achieve that distinction. The popularity of "Teardrops" brought fame to someone in addition to Taylor—her one-time crush, Drew Hardwick. He was probably pretty surprised to hear his own name coming out of the radio. Other Hendersonville residents recognized his name, too, and soon Hendersonville High students were buying Taylor's album just to see if there were any songs about them on it. "The funny thing is, there are so many people in the town where I live, Hendersonville, that think they do have a song written about 'em. You go out into this big world and you go on tour with all these people, and you go back and it's still a small town and they still gossip about it. I think it's one of everybody's favorite things to talk about—who my songs are written about. There are definitely a few more people who think that I've written songs about them than there actually are," Taylor laughingly told *Entertainment Weekly*.

Shortly after the release of her second single, in June of 2007, Taylor and her family drove to downtown Nashville to the convention center for what they thought was another gold record presentation ceremony. Taylor's debut album had gone gold in February and she had already been presented with one gold album, so she was a little confused as to why there was going to be a second ceremony. Little did Taylor know that she was in for a big surprise. During the ceremony, instead of a gold plaque, a representative from the Recording Industry Association of America handed her a platinum plaque, meaning that her album had sold over 1 million copies. When she saw the plaque, she turned to Scott Borchetta, her label president and the organizer of the ceremony, and shouted, "Scott, you liar!" It was quite the feat for Scott to pull one over on Taylor, who is always on top of everything having to do with her career. "I would have been happy to get another gold record, but it was a platinum record. It's the most beautiful thing that I think I've ever seen my life. When I was a little kid, I went to a Kenny Chesney concert and just thought, 'If I can have a platinum album, I'll be set and I'll be satisfied with what I've done.' Here it is and it's such an amazing feeling," Taylor gushed to Musiccitymoms.com. "It's just crazy that in just under eight months we were able to go platinum. Eight months is not a very long time at all. Seeing how people have rallied behind me like this, it's breathtaking, really. I can't comprehend that a million people are out there flying my flag and being awesome and buying my record." Scott Borchetta was convinced that going platinum in eight months was just the beginning for Big Machine Records' star, and is counting on Taylor's debut going triple platinum before her second album is released in 2008.

Taylor released her third single, "Our Song," in the fall of 2007, and it quickly became her biggest hit to date, topping the Billboard Hot Country Song chart before the end of 2007. It was Taylor's first number 1 single and her third top 10 single in one year! "Our Song" also hit number 15 on the Billboard Hot Digital Songs chart in 2007. It went gold in January 2008, and also hit number 16 on the Billboard Hot 100 chart and number 28 on the Billboard Pop 100 chart in February 2008. "Our Song" seems to be a favorite with fans, and its popularity certainly helped propel *Taylor Swift* even further up the charts.

By the end of 2007, Taylor had hit two more very important musical milestones—her debut album had gone double platinum, selling over 2 million copies, and had hit number 1 on Billboard's Top Country chart, making country music history. Taylor was officially the only female country music artist to ever write or cowrite all of the songs on a double-platinum, number 1, debut album. Her album spent more than sixty-six consecutive weeks on the Top Country chart and more than twelve straight weeks in the number 1 spot. Taylor was officially the breakout country star of 2007, and while her album and singles had been burning up the charts, Taylor had spent most of that year out on tour performing and thanking her fans for helping make her number 1.

Chapter 8
Her Boots Were Made For Walking

Going on tour was a dream come true for Taylor. She got to perform and introduce herself to new fans. "I've learned that when you write a song, not everyone hears it right away. I have to introduce myself and play it for one person at a time, and when I want to sell 500,000 albums, I have to meet 500,000 people," Taylor told the *Denver Westword*. She started out with a six-month radio tour to promote "Tim McGraw." This did a lot to help boost the amount of playtime her single got on the radio, but it didn't give her many chances to perform live, so she was thrilled when Rascal Flatts asked her to join them on tour.

Rascal Flatts' "Me and My Gang" Tour was one of the hottest tickets of 2006. The country trio, known for its tight harmonies and mix of pop, country, and rock, is made up of Gary LeVox, Jay DeMarcus, and Joe

Don Rooney. The group was on tour to promote their third number 1 album, *Me and My Gang*, and they sold out most of their performances. Taylor joined the tour in October 2006 and stayed with them through the end of the year. Taylor played her heart out every night, and learned a lot about touring from the seasoned veterans, including what it felt like to have fans really treat her like a star. "I'm still in the 'Oh-my-gosh-this-is-really-happening' phase. After all these concerts that I do, people line up and want me to sign things. I still haven't been able to grasp the fact that if I sign a piece of paper, it might mean something to somebody," Taylor told CMT.com. It was the perfect first tour for Taylor and it set the tone for her future travels.

After Christmas at home, Taylor was on the road again, opening for country legend George Strait for two-and-a-half months. George Strait was a country superstar before Taylor was even born. He has had over fifty number 1 hits and sold more than 62 million copies of his thirteen multi-platinum, thirty platinum, and thirty-three gold albums! "With George Strait, I feel I'm lucky to be in front of a more traditional country audience," Taylor told CMT.com. The crowds' respect for Strait and his music, she told CMT.com, was "like religion." After getting the chance to experience that level of intense fan devotion, Taylor was ready to experience another of country music's legendary traditions.

On April 9, 2007, Taylor stepped out onto country music's most famous stage at the Grand Ole Opry. The tradition of the Grand Ole Opry started in 1925 as live Saturday-night broadcasts from the Ryman Auditorium for WSM Radio. The Opry has introduced America to most of country music's greats, and an appearance there is a sure sign that an artist has finally made it. Wearing a short, teal sequined dress, Taylor gave a powerful performance. She was humbled to sing on the same stage which Dolly Parton, Patsy Cline, Hank Williams, Johnny Cash had made their own.

Next Taylor set out on a tour that was more like

being at a summer camp than work. She joined Jack
Ingram, Kellie Pickler, and headliner Brad Paisley
on Brad's "Bonfire and Amplifiers" tour for about
five months. Brad Paisley personally requested
Taylor for his tour after hearing her album. As he
told *Entertainment Weekly*, "Taylor Swift was one that I
called my manager when I heard her album and said,
'We have to get her out on tour.' And for her to have
written that record at 16, it's crazy how good it is. I
figured I'd hear it and think, 'Well, it's good for 16'—
but it's just flat-out good for any age." Brad wasn't
disappointed by that decision. Taylor fit right in with
everyone, despite the differences in their ages. She
and Kellie became close friends and the two girls had
a fantastic time goofing around and playing pranks.
Brad is a notorious prankster, but Kellie and Taylor
decided to get him before he could play one on them.
"We pranked him first, all the opening acts. You can go
on MySpace and watch it. You know how his single is
called 'Ticks'? I went online and I ordered these giant

tick costumes—like big, giant sumo-wrestler-looking tick costumes—and me and Kellie dressed up in them and ran out on stage and started dancing all around him. And then Jack Ingram, the other opening act, came out in this white exterminator suit halfway through the song, with a sprayer, and proceeded to kill us on stage," Taylor told *Entertainment Weekly*. The high-energy tour was a hit with Taylor's fans, most of whom are also fans of the other acts.

Taylor did take a brief break from "Bonfires and Amplifiers" to perform a few shows with Kenny Chesney in June. Sugarland was one of his other opening acts, and Taylor loves them. Like Jennifer Nettles, Sugarland's powerhouse singer, Taylor likes performing covers of unexpected songs, like Beyonce's "Irreplaceable." Taylor also learned a lot about bantering with a crowd and really working the stage from watching Sugarland and Kenny Chesney.

After her time on the road with Kenny, another of Taylor's personal dreams came true. She got to go on tour with Tim McGraw and Faith Hill. It was a short engagement, but it was a huge thrill for Taylor. Tim and Faith are both country megastars whose music has inspired millions of fans. They didn't have an opening act on their "Soul2Soul" tour, so Taylor performed as a special guest. Taylor's fans definitely enjoyed getting to see her sing "Tim McGraw" while sharing the stage with him.

Taylor finished off 2007 touring with Brad Paisley again. By November, when the tour finally wrapped, Taylor had been on the road for almost a solid year. "There's definitely a feeling of it all being a blur every once in a while," Taylor told the *Ontario Star*. But it was all worth it. The touring helped her performance skills and gave her a chance to personally thank the fans who had supported her from the beginning. It also gave her an opportunity to see a lot of different places. As she told the *Ontario Star*, "It definitely rounds you out as a human . . . I feel like I've already gone to college . . . as far as being away from home, having to learn how

Taylor Swift

Taylor goes glam to perform "Our Song."

Looking lovely at the CMA Awards.

Carrie Underwood presents Taylor with her 2007 CMT Music Awards Breakthrough Video of the Year award.

Taylor performs for her fans.

Taylor shows off her Breakthrough Video of the Year award for "Tim McGraw" at the 2007 CMT Music Awards.

Taylor at the 2008 Grammy Awards
nominations press conference.

to survive, having to learn so many different things about the (music) industry and meeting different people you've never met before."

Taylor had always been a mature teenager, but her mother still accompanies her when she's on the road and her father stays home with Austin. "It's a lot of work helping Tay pursue a music career, but it's a lot of fun, too," Andrea told Searay.com. The mother and daughter manage to get along fairly well on the road, as Taylor explained to GACtv.com. "This is going to sound horrible but the only real argument that I have with my mom is, the temperature on the tour bus. She likes it freezing, and I don't. I like the bus really, really hot. So usually, she'll turn the bus temperature all the way down to 65, and be like, 'Taylor! You've got to stop turning it up!' and then I'll be like, 'Okay Mom.' When she turns around to walk away I'll turn it back to 80. Then she'll come back and be like, 'Taylor!' So those are the only real arguments that we get in. My mom and I really get along and my dad and I get along really well so it's gotten to the point where all we argue about is stupid stuff."

For 2008, Big Machine Records bought their star a brand-new custom tour bus—it even has a treadmill in it! And Taylor has stocked it with all of her favorite things. "Some of my must-have items are makeup—I love makeup. It's not that I absolutely need it, but I really like it. I think it's fun. It's like art class. Also I like my cell phone, just because I like keeping in touch with people. I always have to be knowing exactly what's going on with my career at that moment. I'm always bothering my record label—'Hey! What's going on today? What are we working on?' I am really annoying. Also, I love keeping in touch with my friends. I have an iPod that I always take with me on the road. Let's see, what else do I take on the road with me a lot? I have these boots that have skulls on them, and then they have a pink bow on the top of the skull. They are really cute. They are Liberty boots and I always take them everywhere with me when I travel,"

Taylor told GACtv.com.

At the beginning of 2008, Taylor went back on the road. She joined Alan Jackson for his "Like Red on a Rose" tour in January and February. Alan Jackson is another country legend that Taylor probably picked up some amazing performance tips from. He's released sixteen albums, sold over 45 million albums, and has had thirty-one number 1 songs, twenty-one of which he wrote. Maybe Taylor will write a song with Alan Jackson next! Then Taylor headed up to Canada for a five-city run in March with her old buddies Rascal Flatts. But Taylor's biggest hope for 2008 is to headline her own tour so she can put everything she's learned traveling with all of these country superstars to good use.

Taylor did take some time off from her tours to make a few special appearances, like performing on the season finale of *America's Got Talent* on August 21, 2007. Fourteen-year-old finalist Julienne Irwin requested to sing a duet with Taylor for the live telecast. "Taylor Swift is a huge inspiration to me! She is not only a great singer, she's a great songwriter as well, and it is truly an honor to have the opportunity to perform with her on stage. I know I'm not the only one inspired by her, and I hope my performance makes her proud!" Julienne told GACtv.com. Each of the finalists got to sing with the performer of their choice, and Taylor was honored to be asked. "I can't wait to sing with Julienne on *America's Got Talent*! She's such a sweetheart, and I'm so unbelievably honored that she chose me as her duet choice. She's got such a powerful voice and her story is so endearing," Taylor told GACtv.com. Unfortunately, Julienne didn't win, but she did have a blast performing with her favorite singer. In addition to appearing on television shows and at concerts, Taylor also got to perform at a number of awards shows—and she even managed to win a few awards in the process!

Chapter 9
Music Video Maven

In between tour dates, Taylor filmed her first music videos. With all of the radio play Taylor was getting, she wasn't too worried about her music videos getting on the air on CMT and GAC, the two television channels devoted to country music. It wasn't difficult for Taylor to get in the groove of filming a video. After all, she is a natural born performer!

The first video that Taylor filmed was for the song "Tim McGraw." The concept for the video was simple—two young teenagers remembering the love they had once shared. It cut between Taylor singing by a lake, a handsome boy driving in his pickup truck, and scenes of the two of them together in the past. By the end of the video, the boy finds a letter from Taylor waiting for him. The video's storyline mimics the story Taylor tells in the song and incorporates plenty of the details she sings about. The actor in the video even looked a lot like the boy Taylor wrote the song about. "His [the actor's] name is Clayton Collins, and I think that he lives in L.A. right now. He was a really sweet guy but definitely not my boyfriend . . . But the guy that 'Tim McGraw' was written about looked a lot like the guy we picked for the video. That was done on purpose. He was really tall with dark hair," Taylor explained to GACtv.com. Fans loved the video and were soon requesting it on video countdowns. The video eventually climbed the charts to hit number 1 on CMT's video charts and then made CMT's top videos of 2007 at number 20. It also set a record by appearing for thirty consecutive weeks on GAC's fan-voted weekly Top 20 music countdown show.

When it came time to record her second music video for "Teardrops on My Guitar," Taylor and her director decided to follow the same formula that had worked the first time. In "Teardrops on My Guitar," Taylor has a crush on a boy named Drew who doesn't know about or return her feelings, and Taylor and the director wanted the video to tell that story. Luckily, Taylor found the perfect boy at one of her concerts in California. Tyler Hilton, a singer and actor who had appeared on the hit show *One Tree Hill* and in films like *Walk the Line*, had admitted he was a Taylor fan in a magazine article. When Taylor saw that, she had her manager send him tickets to a show. "I found out he was a fan of my music and he came to my show. I met him in the 'meet and greet' line, and we become friends. He came onstage with me at the show, and I asked him in front of the crowd, 'Do you want to be in my video?' and he said, 'Yeah!'" Taylor told *Country Standard Time*. Tyler was a perfect choice to play Drew. With his tousled hair and chiseled features, he was instantly believable as the high school hotshot who didn't notice that his beautiful best friend liked him. They set the video in a high school and cut between scenes of Taylor and "Drew" goofing off with scenes of Taylor, dressed in a beautiful gown, lying alone on her bed holding her guitar. Taylor and Tyler had a blast filming together and are still friends. He loves going to her shows, and whenever he's there she invites him up onstage to sing with her. The video for "Teardrops On My Guitar" did incredibly well on the country channels CMT and GAC, but it also made it into the Top 20 countdown on VH1 and went into rotation on notoriously anti-country MTV. Taylor had her first crossover video hit—and it was only her second single! It was even voted the number 10 video for all of 2007 on CMT.

For the video for "Our Song," Taylor decided to change things up and skip casting a boy altogether! It opens with Taylor, wearing shorts and a tank top with her hair straightened, painting her toenails and chatting on the phone, and cuts between that and Taylor in several other scenes. In one, she is wearing a blue dress with a full skirt and singing on a porch. In another, she is wearing a bright orange floor-length gown and laying in a bed of multicolored roses, and in the last scene, she's in a little black dress, rocking out with her entire band. In the last scene, Taylor is strumming a brand-new guitar that's as dressed up as she is—the entire face is covered in glittering rhinestones! Taylor's fans began voting for the video immediately. After only a few weeks, "Our Song" made it to number 1 on both CMT and GAC.

But her music videos weren't the first television appearances for Taylor. In the summer of 2006, Taylor's pursuit of stardom was the subject of a part-documentary series called *GAC Short Cuts* that aired on the Great American Country channel. The series gave Taylor's fans a chance to see Taylor at home, at school, hanging out with her friends, and promoting her album. The crew followed her into her high school to watch her perform a song she'd just written for the school talent show called "I'd Lie," into the studio for a recording session, to New York City to perform on *Good Morning America*, to the concert where she was opening for George Strait, and at home on a rare day off with her family. The six-episode series was the perfect way to introduce spunky Taylor to fans of country music, and it helped make Taylor more comfortable on camera. Her honesty, enthusiasm, and tendency to wear her heart on her sleeve endeared her to fans. With that kind of on-screen charisma, there's sure to be many more award-winning music videos in Taylor's future.

Chapter 10
Awards

There is nothing more satisfying for musicians than to be recognized for their work by their peers and fans at an awards show. 2007 was the first year that Taylor was eligible for any awards and once nominations were announced for all of the major country music awards, Taylor kept a running countdown in her head of the upcoming shows. She was nervous and excited and absolutely thrilled to be nominated for any awards.

Her first big show was the 2007 CMT Music Awards on April 16 at Belmont University's Curb Event Center. Taylor was nominated in two categories: the Buckle Breakthrough Video of the Year award and the Female Video of the Year award. Taylor arrived at the awards show wearing a beautiful white dress with graduated silver sequins covering the bodice and skirt, ready to discover whether or not she had won. She had tried not to get her hopes up too high, so she was shocked when she heard her name announced as the winner of the Breakthrough Video award. She ran up to the podium, flushed with excitement, and accepted her trophy from 2006's winner, Carrie Underwood. "I cannot believe this is happening right now. This is for my MySpace people and the fans," Taylor said, holding up her trophy. Taylor didn't win the Female Video of the Year award, but she didn't mind at all. "The highlight of my career so far has been winning the CMT Breakthrough Video of the Year award. It's a fan-voted awards show, so I don't see any greater honor than winning an award that was voted on by fans. It was for my first video that I ever put out ['Tim McGraw'], and I'll never forget the feeling of just running . . . bolting up to that stage. It was just the most amazing feeling," Taylor explained to Music.aol.com. Since it was her first award, it was extra special to Taylor, as she told the *Tennessean*. "I can't explain the feeling. I had never been nominated for anything before. I had won nothing before, literally nothing. To have my name called, I didn't know what that was like. I didn't think I was going to get it. When my name was called, I just ran up to the stage at, like, 100 miles an hour." That night and that award will probably always be especially important to Taylor, since that was the night when she really felt that she had made it in country music.

For her next awards show, the Academy of Country Music Awards in Las Vegas, Nevada, on May 15, 2007, Taylor was nominated for Top New Female Vocalist. She was also on deck to perform her single, "Tim McGraw," for the packed venue full of country music superstars and legends, including Tim McGraw himself. "It was unbelievable, I was performing on stage and it was just me and my guitar. After my song, I stepped down and said, 'Hi, I'm Taylor.' I hadn't met him in the entire year my single had been out. So it was just really cool," Taylor told the *Pantagraph*. Taylor lost to Carrie Underwood that night, but it would always be special to Taylor, anyway, because she finally got to meet the man whose music had inspired her first hit single.

On October 16, 2007, Taylor won a very prestigious award that very few stars are ever even nominated for—the Songwriter/Artist of the Year award from the Nashville Songwriters Association International. She actually tied with Alan Jackson for the award, and they were both honored that night. Taylor was the youngest artist to ever win the award and she didn't mind sharing the spotlight at all! "I am just freaking out. I'm so excited because I got a publishing deal when I was 14 and every single day was devoted to writing songs. And it was before I got a record deal, it was before any of this started. I was a songwriter in town. And the fact that this award is voted on by my songwriter peers—I don't even know how to explain how honored I feel. I mean, I was sitting at the table and they called Alan Jackson's name and I'm just like, 'Oh my God! That's awesome!' And then all of the sudden they say my name and I'm like, 'What happened?' I'm so humbled by this experience. It's just so unbelievable," Taylor told GACtv.com. Alan was so impressed by his cowinner that he invited Taylor to open for him on his next tour, which was almost as exciting for Taylor as it was to win the award!

But nothing could top the next award Taylor received. On November 7, 2007, Taylor attended the Country Music Association Awards at the Sommet Center in Nashville, Tennessee. Taylor wore a stunning metallic gold dress with a fitted bodice and a full, cascading skirt. The event was televised nationally on ABC, and Taylor got the chance to perform her third single, "Our Song," for the crowd. She changed into the short black sequined dress, black tights, and long black gloves that she had worn in her music video for the same song, and strummed along on her rhinestone-covered guitar as she sang her heart out. The crowd was blown away by her performance, but Taylor was blown away when her name was announced as the winner of the prestigious Horizon Award. The Horizon Award is always given to a new country singer or group that has left a lasting impact on the industry. "I can't even believe this; this is definitely the highlight of my senior year," Taylor said as she accepted her trophy. It was a huge honor to win that award and Taylor was completely in awe of her success.

Taylor was also nominated for Favorite Female Country Artist at the American Music Awards, but she lost to Carrie Underwood on November 18, 2007. Taylor was just excited to have been nominated and hadn't expected to win, since she had some pretty stiff competition from Martina McBride and Carrie Underwood. Taylor looked adorable that night, though, wearing a short, black, sixties-inspired dress accented along the neck and front with metallic studs. She paired the dress with her favorite pair of black cowboy boots and enjoyed getting the chance to hang out in Los Angeles before and after the show.

Taylor received her most exciting nomination of the year bright and early on the morning of December 6, 2007. At only seventeen years old, Taylor was the youngest artist on the stage at the 50th Annual Grammy nomination announcement press conference. She was sharing the spotlight that morning with some pretty illustrious company, including Dave Grohl and Taylor Hawkins of the Foo Fighters, Fergie, Akon, Quincy Jones, Linkin Park, and George Lopez. "I'm starstruck," Taylor admitted to *People*. She was very honored to be asked to help present the nominations for the biggest awards ceremony in the music industry.

The Grammy Awards encompass every genre of music, from country to hip-hop to pop to indie rock, making these nominations some of the most coveted. There are specific categories for every genre, and a few awards that acts from every genre compete for, such as Best New Artist. Ready to shine that morning, Taylor wore a simple black dress and read off her assigned nominations with her usual bubbly enthusiasm. Then Dave Grohl and Taylor Hawkins of the quirky rock group the Foo Fighters took the podium to announce the nominees for Best New Artist. Taylor was shocked to hear Dave announce her name. She instantly squealed with excitement, rushed over to Dave Grohl and Taylor Hawkins, and gave them both huge hugs. "Don't worry, Taylor, you got it in the bag," Dave said as he hugged her back. All of the veteran musicians onstage were charmed by Taylor's enthusiasm. George Lopez got so caught up in the moment that he gave her a big hug, too. "I've always been a hugger. I honestly did not think I was going to get nominated, so when they said my name I just felt like hugging somebody. I'm glad that everyone started hugging. If we all hugged more, the world would be a better place," Taylor told *People*. After everyone shared a laugh and finished hugging, they got on with the nominations, but Taylor was still in awe. "It absolutely blows me away that these people even know my name and can pronounce it right," Taylor told Music.aol.com.

Taylor was especially pleased to be nominated for the Best New Artist award, since many of the previous winners have gone on to have some of the most successful careers in music, including The Beatles, Alicia Keys, Sheryl Crow, Taylor's idol LeAnn Rimes, and 2007's winner, Taylor's friend Carrie Underwood. "It's so unbelievable. That's an all-genre category, and there's certainly no obligation to have a country artist in the category," Taylor told the *Houston Chronicle*.

The 50th annual Grammy Awards were held at the Staples Center in Los Angeles on the night of February 10, 2008, and were broadcast live on CBS. Taylor looked stunning as she worked the red carpet wearing a strapless purple gown with a flowing skirt and leaf detailing. Her blond, corkscrew curls hung loosely down her back and she positively glowed with anticipation. Unfortunately for Taylor, Amy Winehouse took home the award that night, but Taylor was thrilled just to have been a part of the prestigious awards show. She did get the chance to make her debut in front of the Grammy audience that night when she appeared as a presenter alongside Juanes for the Best Rap Song Collaboration. Taylor joked with her copresenter and charmed the crowd. Then she presented the award to Rihanna and Jay-Z for "Umbrella," which just happens to be one of Taylor's favorite songs to cover at her concerts.

Just at the starting line of what promises to be a long and successful career, Taylor isn't bothered by losses when it comes to awards. She feels lucky and honored to be nominated, especially when she is competing against stars that she idolized growing up. Besides, Taylor isn't slowing down anytime soon. So she is sure to be nominated for many more awards in the future.

Chapter 11
Merry Christmas

Taylor has always loved Christmas, but she got into the spirit extra early in 2007 when she recorded her holiday album, *Sounds of the Season: The Taylor Swift Holiday Collection* in July. Taylor wrote a few original holiday tunes, but also put her own spin on classics like "Silent Night," "Santa Baby," and "White Christmas." The album was released exclusively in Target stores on October 16, 2007, and it was the best Christmas gift Taylor could have given her eager fans.

The holiday album did very well. It hit number 46 on the Billboard 200 chart and number 14 on Billboard's Top Country Album chart. Singles from the album also did fairly well on Billboard's Hot Country Songs chart. "White Christmas" hit number 59, "Silent Night" peaked at number 54, Taylor's original composition "Christmases When You Were Mine" made it to number 48, the ever popular "Santa Baby" hit number 43, and "Last Christmas" made it all the way to number 28. Not bad for a holiday album sold in only one chain store!

In addition to *Sounds of the Season*, Taylor released a second special album on November 6, 2007—*Taylor Swift: Deluxe Limited Edition*. Taylor was itching to give her fans new music, but her label wanted her to wait a little longer before her next album. As a compromise, they repackaged her debut with some amazing extras and a few new songs. As Taylor explained to Music.aol.com, "The album has been out for a year, but it's too early to put out the second studio album. But we wanted to give [the fans] more music. So this was an opportunity to put out three new songs and a bunch of exclusive content. I actually edited a home movie on my laptop, and it's on there as a special feature. There's my first phone conversation with Tim McGraw, all my music videos and a bunch of concert footage. The [new] songs are demos that I wrote when

I was 15, trying to get a record deal."

The new songs on the album are "Invisible," a song about a girl who is in love with a boy who is in love with another girl who doesn't know he exists; "A Perfectly Good Heart," a bittersweet song about suffering through first heartbreak; and "I'm Only Me When I'm With You," an upbeat happy song about young love and how all-consuming it can be. Taylor wrote all three of the bonus songs and, while they didn't make it onto her album originally, they were good enough to land her a record deal with Big Machine Records. Fans loved the bonus material and the three extra songs are some of the most downloaded of all of Taylor's songs on iTunes. Taylor was very glad that those three songs got a second life with the release of the bonus album, as all three were very personal tunes that she had always looked forward to sharing with her fans.

Chapter 12
All About Taylor

When Taylor isn't on tour or in the studio, she's just another teenager who loves hanging out with her friends and giggling about boys, eating junk food, and going to the mall. Taylor's horrible at sports, but loves doing yoga, and she's completely addicted to *Law & Order: SVU*, *CSI*, and *Grey's Anatomy*. Her lucky number is thirteen, and she is superstitous about it, as she explained to the *Philadelphia Inquirer*. "I was born on Dec. 13, and I turned 13 on Friday the 13th. And from the point where my album was released until it went platinum was exactly 13 months." The outgoing message on her cell phone even sounds just like any other teenager's. "Hey, it's Taylor. I can't get your call right now but call back like 100 times and I'll get back to you," Scott Borchetta, the head of her record label told GACtv.com. But unlike a lot of teenagers, you won't find Taylor out at wild parties or sneaking into bars. "I'm just really more of a laid-back person. I've never been a party girl," Taylor explained to *Entertainment Weekly*.

Even during her off-hours, Taylor knows that her fans will be watching to see what she does. And that's fine with her, because Taylor isn't like a lot of other stars her age. "When I'm about to make decisions, my point of reference is the 6-year-old girl in the front row of my concert. I think about what she would think if she saw me do what I was considering doing. Then I go back and I think about her mom and what her mom would think if I did that," Taylor told *Entertainment Weekly*. Taylor has never given in to peer pressure to do anything. She's in no hurry to grow up, and, as far as she is concerned, there shouldn't be room in any kid's life for drugs or alcohol.

So what does Taylor do for fun if she's not out all night at parties? Well, Taylor loves spending time on Old Hickory Lake with her family. They have two boats, a 420 Sundancer and a 220 Sundeck, and they spend a lot of sunny days boating. But Taylor's best friend, Abigail Anderson, is who she likes to spend most of her time off with. "I have every Sunday off, so I usually spend it with her," Taylor told GACtv.com. The girls like to bake goodies and watch their favorite movie, *Napoleon Dynamite*, over and over. They also like to prank their ex-boyfriends with funny phone calls.

There are some exes, though, that Taylor would rather not see, like Drew Hardwick, Taylor's one-time crush and the inspiration for the song, "Teardrops on My Guitar." Since he lives in Hendersonville, she couldn't avoid him forever after her song came out, although she tried. Taylor told *Seventeen* that Drew called her after the single was released, but that she was too nervous to call him back. Eventually he showed up at her house to see her in person. "Kellie Pickler and I were going to a hockey game and this guy pulls up. I didn't have my contacts on and didn't see him right away. He's a little older, a little taller, the guy I wrote that song about 2 1/2 years ago. I hadn't talked to him. I didn't know what to say and here he is walking toward me," Taylor told the *Miami Herald*. But it wasn't nearly as bad as she thought it was going to be to discuss her now-public crush on Drew. "Everything was nice. There was no, like, screaming and 'You're too late!' It was all very cordial," Taylor told Nashville's WKRN Radio. It would have been funny if Drew and Taylor had finally gotten together, but Taylor moved on a long time ago!

As far as boyfriends go, all of the romance in Taylor's life remains in the past. "I'm completely single!" Taylor told Music.aol.com. "I think that love is something that hits you when you're not looking for it. So I've been actively not looking for it for like two years. I'm always the third wheel on my friends' dates. I have a bunch of best friends who never go more than a month without having a boyfriend. And I think that's kinda rubbed off on me, because I've seen the stuff they've gone through over the past two years. And I'm just like, 'I'm gonna pursue my career instead.'" Taylor has thousands of male fans who would love a chance to get to know the beautiful starlet a little better, but Taylor just isn't interested in finding love at the moment. "I've been in relationships and I thought I was in love. I've never had a love for anything that was enough to make me stop thinking about music. I've been in relationships but there was always something that I needed more. It never filled something that I felt like I was missing. Music is the only thing that could do that. Maybe I'm un-datable right now. I've been going through this independent phase where I haven't been interested in dating at all," she explained to GACtv.com. Taylor's future boyfriends better watch out, though, since she has a habit of singing about her relationships in her songs, and she's not shy about naming names! Hopefully someday Taylor will find a guy who only inspires happy love songs.

Since Taylor just graduated from high school, and spent her junior and senior years being homeschooled, there's no real chance she'll meet a boy in study hall. But she didn't really miss going to a regular high school. "I don't think there's really anything I miss, to be honest. There's a lot less drama when you're touring the country on a major tour. And I've actually been to prom before . . . twice. So I don't want anyone to feel bad for me. It was really great that I got to experience those first two years of high school, and I'll never forget that. I learned a lot. But I feel like I've had the best senior year ever," Taylor told Music.aol.com.

She kept up with her classes on the road and graduated with the rest of her class in June of 2008. "I do my homeschooling in the mornings usually, then I'll go to meet-and-greets and sound checks. But morning is the only free time I have," Taylor explained to the *Pantagraph*. One big benefit of homeschooling was that Taylor got the chance to do more creative assignments than she used to. For one of her English papers, she wrote about the country music group Little Big Town. As she told GACtv.com, "I wrote this ten-page paper about them. When it came time to get a gift for them for their platinum album party, I just printed out my report and gave it to them!" Taylor's report was probably the most unique gift that Little Big Town has ever received!

Taylor isn't usually big on parties, but she has been known to make an exception or two over the years. She was busy recording her debut album when she turned sixteen and she didn't get a chance to have a "sweet sixteen" party like most girls her age. So, for her eighteenth birthday, Taylor's parents threw her the girliest, pinkest birthday bash that Nashville had ever seen at local hotspot Lot 7. She spent the day registering to vote and getting ready for the party with her closest friends from high school. She chose a hot-pink Betsey Johnson dress to wear that night. "It was between this and a black dress, but I knew all my friends would be in black, so I went with the pink. I love pink!" Taylor told *People*. Pink was certainly the color of the night. The whole club was decked out with pink balloons and lights. There was even a photo booth with a pink background! But the biggest pink moment of the night came when Scott Borchetta, president of Taylor's music label, presented her with her birthday gift, a pink Chevrolet pickup truck. There were over two hundred guests at the party, including fellow country crooners Kellie Pickler, Chuck Wicks, Lady Antebellum, and Big & Rich's John Rich, who led the crowd in singing "Happy Birthday." But Taylor's favorite birthday gift couldn't be wrapped. "What I really wanted for my birthday was a number 1 record, and I got that, too!" Taylor told *People*.

There are definitely times that Taylor can't pretend she's a normal teenager, like when a fan asked her to sign an autograph on the side of the road after a car accident. "Yeah, somebody hit my car and then asked me to sign a broken piece of my taillight," Taylor told Jam.canoe.ca. "Then it was crazy. Five minutes later this other woman saw me on the side of the road and decided that she wanted to get an autograph for her daughter. So she pulled over to get my autograph and then somebody hit her car. It was quite the experience." Luckily Taylor has an excellent sense of humor and is able to laugh at herself when strange things happen because of her stardom. She knows she'll never be a normal teenager again, but she wouldn't trade in even one second of her amazing career to be back in homeroom hoping to make it big someday. She's managed to stay the same sweet, grounded, hard-working girl she's always been, thanks to good friends and a loving family, and it seems like Taylor might just be one star who can have it all—the great career and a happy, mostly normal home life!

Chapter 13
What's Next

Taylor has had an exhausting ride since she signed her record deal with Big Machine Records. She'd been on multiple tours, released a debut album, floated three hit singles, watched her album go double platinum, won several awards, and made country music history. That's not too shabby—especially since that was all before she graduated from high school! For a lot of people, it would be time for a vacation, but not Taylor.

Taylor has been busy in the studio recording her next album. "I am so excited about it. There is so much I wanted to put on the first album, I can't even wait. I am so excited about giving these people who have done so much for me and have had the (first) album this entire time something new to latch on to. They've been so supportive of these 12 songs of mine, I want to give them more," Taylor told the *Pantagraph*. She's hoping to release the album in the fall of 2008.

Taylor has been working with some different songwriters to make sure that her new songs are fresh and exciting. John Rich of Big & Rich and Colbie Caillat are just two of her new partners. With Colbie, Taylor wrote the song "Breath" which she says is about losing a close friendship. "I'm extremely excited about the song I wrote with Colbie. It's so my favorite thing on the record already . . . It's got a very cool vibe about it. It's hard to put my finger on it—it's a moment," Taylor told the *Kalamazoo Gazette*.

Taylor is sticking to subject matter she knows firsthand for her new songs—that means boys, crushes, and friendships. One thing Taylor won't be writing about is being famous. "I'm not going to write songs about what it's like being on the road. I know 99 percent of my fans can't relate to that. I will write songs about things I can relate to and the people buying my album can relate to," Taylor told the *Miami Herald*. Taylor wants to make sure that she writes songs her fans will want to listen to over and over again. As she explained to the *Pantagraph*, "I think to succeed over a long period of time, you have to not reflect back on the success you have so far. For the second album, I am going to make it like the first album. I am going to put out eight songs I think can be singles, not just three or four. Record companies want you to only put three or four great songs on an album, with the rest filler, so [as] not to waste a single. But I want to put out great songs for people. As long as I am making people as happy as they are making me, I will feel like I've accomplished something."

One thing Taylor and her fans are hoping for in the near future is a Taylor Swift tour. Taylor has toured with some of the biggest names in country music, so she would be sure to put on an amazing show as a headliner. And it's certainly one of Taylor's biggest goals, as she told the *St. Petersburg Times*. "Well, in five years, I will be 22 going on 23. I see myself living in a little house, an old house that's really pretty and decorated really cute. But I won't see it a lot because I want to stay on the road and I want to be headlining. That's my dream, to be on a headlining tour, because that means you've got longevity and you've got thousands of people that are willing to come out and see you every night." It probably won't take Taylor five years to achieve that dream if her second album is as successful as her first!

As things calm down, Taylor would like to return to her roots and do some songwriting for other artists. While on tour with Brad Paisley, Taylor became friends with Kellie Pickler, another new country artist. When Kellie got some bad news out on the road, Taylor helped her deal with it. "Kellie came on my bus this summer and was all upset about her ex-boyfriend. She was like, 'I just want to be over this!' And she gets up on stage now and tells everyone all about it. And I'm like, 'Okay, if you want to tell everyone your personal stuff, but there's no better way to get over something than to write it all down.' So we went into the back bedroom of my tour bus and wrote this awesome song. It's about how, for the rest of his life, he's going to

regret cheating on her. And she's said to me since then,
'You know what, I didn't think there was anything I
could do to really get past that. But writing that song
gave me complete closure,'" Taylor told Music.aol.com.
Taylor loved writing a song from someone else's point
of view, as she explained to CMT.com. ". . . it was so
cool jumping into someone else's feelings for a minute
and writing from their perspective. It was like I was
writing my very first song. Exhilarating."

One thing Taylor has already been doing is giving
back to her community. Taylor has been known to
give her phone number out to fans she meets who are
going through a hard time and she spends what little
free time she has answering fan mail, but that's not
enough for her. As a huge MySpace fan, Taylor loves
connecting with people online, but she also knows that
the Internet can be a very dangerous place for kids.
So she teamed up with Phil Bredesen, the governor
of Tennessee, for a statewide program called "Delete
Online Predators." The goal of the program is to

educate middle-school students and their parents about safe Internet use. Taylor's goal is for all students to sign the NetSmartz "Internet Safety Pledge," a promise to protect themselves online developed by the National Center for Missing and Exploited Children. "Chatting with friends and surfing the Internet is cool. But it's important to stay safe. Be smart about keeping your identity private online," Taylor told *That's Country*. The campaign includes school visits, distribution of brochures with tips for online safety, distribution of NetSmartz Safety Pledge brochures with a special message from Taylor, and wristband giveaways.

Taylor also performed in the Sprint Speed and Sound Concert to benefit the Victory Junction Gang Camp, a children's charity that helps kids with terminal diseases. "They have camps all over the country for kids who are sick. It's one week . . . they forget they're sick and just have a blast and hang out with other people who they can relate to. They look forward to it, and I love that cause," Taylor explained to People.com.

She even made a very special donation to the charity on January 10, 2008—her birthday present from her label, a pink Chevy pickup truck. "My label was so awesome to give me this amazing truck for my birthday. The moment I saw it, in all its pink glory, I knew that the kids at the Victory Junction Gang Camp would love it," Taylor explained to Frontstretch.com. Causes that affect children are dear to Taylor and you can be sure she'll be involved in many more of them in the future.

Taylor's career is on fire, she's got family and friends who love her, and she's working toward accomplishing many more of the goals she's set for herself, but is there anything she'd like to do that she's going to miss out on? Most of Taylor's friends are heading off for college, while Taylor is putting aside thoughts of higher education for a while. "Of course, you're always going to wonder about the road not taken, the dorm not taken, and the sorority not taken. But if I wasn't doing this, I would've missed out on the best moments I've ever known and the most wonderful life that I still can't believe I get to live. I'm still friends with the same people I was friends with in high school, and I feel like I haven't changed as a person," Taylor explained to CMT.com.

She does plan to continue her education when time permits, as she told the *St. Petersburg Times*. "I would love to take a class every once in a while, but I really cannot walk away from this for four years. Four years is a long time. People will fill your spot." Taylor has been getting a different kind of education than her peers by working in the business that she loves. "I think anyone, when they come across something that fascinates them more than anything they've ever seen—and that's what music does for me—I think when each person finds that in their life, that's when they become driven," Taylor explained to the *Philadelphia Inquirer*. "That's when they grow up. I was just kind of a fluke in that I found mine at age 10. I was like: I found this. There's no way I can let it go."

Taylor certainly hopes she'll have a long and

successful career, but she doesn't really want to be compared to anyone. "You know, I'm not really looking to model my career after anyone. I'm looking to do something new. I want to do everything new. I mean country music will always be country music . . . but the audiences can be changed and expanded. I think it would be great if when I'm 90 years old and looking back on life, I can say I did things people didn't expect and was successful," Taylor told GACtv.com. Don't worry, Taylor—you've already changed country music for the better!

Chapter 14
Country Style

One of the coolest things about Taylor is her unique style. If you want to make Taylor's style your own, start with a good pair of cowboy boots. Taylor's favorite pair is made of sky-blue leather and they add three inches to her height! They have red and pink detailing and a big heart on the front of each, with "Taylor" written on the right foot and "Swift" on the left. Taylor's boot collection is huge! She wears them with every type of outfit, from fancy dresses to blue jeans. "When you pair a dress with cowboy boots, it's kind of a cool irony to the outfit," Taylor told the *Houston Chronicle*.

Taylor loves dresses. Her favorites are sundresses in summer and tights or leggings with cozy sweater dresses in winter. She loves fabrics that are comfortable and easy to move in. One thing you won't find her wearing is anything too sexy. In Taylor's opinion, it's best to leave some things to the imagination!

When it comes to accessorizing, Taylor likes to wear big sparkly earrings, delicate silver chains, multiple bracelets, and headbands. She's never without her leather bracelet with the words "Love Love Love" embossed on it. Taylor keeps most of her makeup very fresh and light, but she loves to experiment with her eyes. She is especially fond of shimmery green, blue, pink, and purple eye shadows and fun eyeliners. As for her beautiful blond hair, "It's been really curly and fro'd out since I was little. I used to fight it. I used to try to straighten it, which turned out horrific. But then I just decided a couple of years ago that I wanted to wear my hair the way that it is. When I'm going on TV, of course, you have the glam squad. They make it look a lot better," Taylor told the *St. Petersburg Times*. For loose curls like Taylor's, try using hot rollers or a curling iron.

For special occasions or performances and appearances, Taylor turns to her personal stylist for help. Sandy Spika has been helping Taylor get stageworthy for a few years and she always makes Taylor look and feel beautiful. For concerts, Sandy chooses girly sundresses and cowboy boots with fun details. But for award shows, Sandy goes all out. "I like really long, one-of-a-kind dresses, dramatic massive dresses that take a lot of effort to walk in," Taylor told the *Houston Chronicle*. Sandy hasn't disappointed her client yet, often designing one-of-a-kind originals for Taylor. Taylor also wears lots of Sandy's designs in her music videos.

Taylor's style epitomizes the all-American girl-next-door, and she'll probably never give up that wholesome, fun image for a racier one. It's just not who she is, and she doesn't ever want to be anyone but herself!

Chapter 15
Swift Taylor Facts

So you think you're Taylor's biggest fan? Well here are the fun facts that every Taylor Swift fan should know by heart!

Full Name: Taylor Alison Swift

Date of Birth: December 13,1989

Hometown: Wyomissing, Pennsylvania

Height: 5'11"

Hair Color: naturally blond and curly

Siblings: younger brother Austin

Parents: Scott and Andrea Swift

Star Sign: Sagittarius

Hobbies: playing guitar, songwriting, boating

Instruments: guitar—a Taylor Grand Auditorium acoustic guitar made of koa wood

Biggest Musical Influences: LeAnn Rimes, Patsy Cline, and her grandmother

Her Lucky Charm: a leather bracelet that says "Love Love Love"

Favorite Stores: BCBG and Forever 21

Favorite Clothing: dresses and cowboy boots

Favorite Tim McGraw Song: "Can't Tell Me Nothin'"

Favorite Ice Cream: vanilla with cookie dough

Pets: a cat named Indi and two Dobermans

Favorite TV Show: *Law & Order, CSI,* and *Grey's Anatomy*

Favorite Color: pink

Favorite Sport to Watch: hockey

Favorite Sports Team: the Nashville Predators and the Tennessee Titans

Favorite Movie: *Love Actually*

Lucky Number: thirteen

If she wasn't a musician she'd like to be: a criminal investigator

Chapter 17
Taylor Online

Taylor Swift is always on the move. So, if you want to keep up with country's golden girl, here is a list of websites with all of the latest Taylor information all the time! Taylor would always want you to be careful online. As an advocate for "Delete Online Predators," she would caution you to never give out any sort of personal information—like your name, address, phone number, or the name of your school or sports team—and to never try to meet someone in person that you met online. When you are surfing the Net, you have to remember that not everything you read there is true. So take online information with a grain of salt. And remember, never surf the Web without your parents' permission. Can't find your favorite website? Websites come and go, so don't worry—there's sure to be another Taylor site to replace it soon!

www.taylorswift.com

This is Taylor's official site. It has updates on her projects, tours, videos, photographs, and an online shop where you can buy official Taylor gear.

www.myspace.com/TaylorSwift

This is Taylor Swift's official MySpace page. She checks her page every day and tries to respond to as many fans as possible. So check it out (with your parent's permission, of course) and leave some love for Taylor!

www.taylorswiftlove.com

This is a totally rockin' Taylor fan site. It has pictures, links, video, lots of news updates, and forums where you can chat about all things Taylor.